On the Chicopee Spur

Other Works by Al Ortolani

Slow Stirring Spoon (chapbook), High/Coo Press, 1981

The Last Hippie of Camp 50, Woodley Press, 1989

Finding the Edge, Woodley Press, 2011

Wren's House, Coal City Press, 2012

Cooking Chili on the Day of the Dead, Aldrich Press, 2013

Waving Mustard in Surrender, NYQ Books, 2014

Francis Shoots Pool at Chubb's Bar, Spartan Press, 2015

Paper Birds Don't Fly, NYQ Books, 2016

Ghost Sign, Co-authored with Adam Jameson, Melissa Fite
            Johnson, and J.T. Knoll, 39 West Press &
            Spartan Press, 2016

On the Chicopee Spur

Poems

Al Ortolani

NYQ Books™

The New York Quarterly Foundation, Inc.
New York, New York

NYQ Books™ is an imprint of The New York Quarterly Foundation, Inc.

The New York Quarterly Foundation, Inc.
P. O. Box 2015
Old Chelsea Station
New York, NY 10113

www.nyq.org

First Edition

Set in New Baskerville

Layout by Raymond P. Hammond

Cover Design by Raymond P. Hammond

Cover Photo: "Thunder Snow," by Blane Reeves,
          Selected by Ava and Rider Middleton

Library of Congress Control Number: 2018935429

ISBN: 978-1-63045-056-4

On the Chicopee Spur

Notes

In *On the Chicopee Spur,* the haibun form allowed me to speak plainly in the bread of prose, and then slice the loaf with haiku. It's the form Basho used to highlight his journeys across Japan in the seventeenth century. Many of the haiku are not written in the traditional 5-7-5 syllable format, but instead, speak tersely in the spirit of the haiku, experimental, American. Some of the subject matter comes from the immediacy of the hospice experience, others from memories and daydreams along the way.

I would like to thank all health workers involved in hospice services for their dedication to their patients, to my family and friends, and to all who joined us in the commons room for Thanksgiving Dinner.

A special thanks to Brian Daldorph, Marjorie Saiser, Michael Dylan Welch, and Ray Rasmussen for their close reading and comments, as well as Raymond Hammond of NYQ Books for his commitment to publishing poetry in all its forms.

And to my wife, Sherri, who understands me better than I do myself.

Contents

poncho over my head

Death is a Sneeze   / 17
On the Chicopee Spur   / 18
Downspout   / 19
Alleyway   / 20
Broad Leaf   / 21
Turquoise Stone   / 22
Pearl Harbor Day   / 23
Remodeling the Cinema   / 24
Helium Balloon   / 25

waking at 3 a.m.

Butterfly Weed   / 29
Green River Soda   / 30
Ghosts in the Creek Bed   / 31
Box of Rags   / 32
Wife and Cat   / 33
Visiting Family   / 34
Oliver Claws the Door   / 35
Suburban Hermit   / 36
William Blake Saw Angels in a Tree   / 37

lightning at midnight,

Sleeping with Magnum   / 41
Spooning   / 42
Faulkner at Christmas   / 43
Scrooge   / 44
Solstice   / 45
Johnson County Exit   / 46

Blue Collar   / 47
Bone Cold   / 48
Frozen   / 49
Key Card Dawn   / 50
Chicken Feet   / 51
My Irish Mother   / 52
Black Beads 1   / 53
Black Beads 2   / 54

winter morning—

Scudding Sky   / 57
Girls' Choir   / 58
Tool Shed   / 59
Through the Screen Door   / 60
Temple of the Ford Ranger   / 61
Charleston Midnight   / 62
First Seed   / 63
Cleaning Out the Rock Garden   / 64
Stonecrop   / 65
Green Painted Walls   / 66
Wall Dogs   / 67
The Story Begins with a Dog   / 68

clouds thread

Brushing Latex on Mrs. Ford's Second Story   / 71
At the Trading Post Bridge   / 72
Orion's Belt   / 73
Spring Snow   / 74
Home Opener   / 75
Shooting Hoops for Beer   / 76

Thieves at Night   / 77
Tailgating at the Last Supper   / 78

old photograph

Monofilament Whiskers   / 81
Grub Worm   / 82
The Styrofoam of Stuff   / 83
Across the Wooden Fence   / 84
Light in the Back of the House   / 85
Passing Period   / 86
Beige Jesus   / 87
Pine Tree Morning   / 88

snow falling

Stone Fence   / 91
Kayaking the Upper Buffalo   / 92
Metal Bailed Bucket   / 93
Last Float Trip on the Gasconade   / 94
Swimming Deer   / 95
Hunting Morels   / 96
Black Bear   / 97

high on Mt. Sneffels

Acknowledgements   / 102

On the Chicopee Spur

For Virginia Sullivan Ortolani,
Dolores Morris Keiter,
and Bonnie Newton Sullivan Morris

poncho over my head
knees to chin
hail rattles the couloir
where I sit
with other stones

Death is a Sneeze

Little poem that makes me no money. Little poem that I
cannot eat or barter for rent. Little poem in the roadside
weeds beside the early asparagus, the first clover bloom. A
short sneeze of haiku, pollen septum. Monkey mind has me
in its grip. I want to hold something, to accumulate, to own.
The job drags. The sky grays. The air cools. Little poem in
my backpack, you are scrawled in pencil. It took a page of
notes to find you, lead scratch marks, margin doodles, a
line, a syllable crossed out, chucked into the mulch pile.
The spring wind cleans the patio. Nothing remains but
three lines. Yesterday, I cut the grass. Today, I'm wearing the
same grass-stained pants, my old shoes double-knotted for
the next step.

april grave,
daughter spreads new seed
         over turned earth

On the Chicopee Spur

My daughters and I pick blackberries in the shadows, the
July night coming on hot and heavy as a canvas awning. The
first lightning bugs blink in and out between thorns. As I
dip my head into the thicket for berries, a man walks slowly
up the tracks, his denim overalls and plaid shirt too heavy
for the evening's heat. He keeps between the rails, minding
his way, watching his shoes, and as he passes, he gives me a
barely perceptible nod of his head. Several times I stop and
watch as he continues over the trestle, the rail line bending
out of town into the bean fields.

deepening
the night between blackberries

Two days later, I read an obituary of a man found dead on
the Chicopee Spur. The grainy photo appears to be that
of the man from blackberry picking. Possibly, it is my over
active imagination, but when he had walked by me, his
features blurred. The light wavered over him like it will over
a mirage.

sewing a button
her fingers
     wait
  the needle's return

I didn't say anything to my daughters. They were too young
for an old man's misfortune or a father's premonition. I
start them slowly on blackberries, immerse them in thorns
and chiggers.

blackbird—releasing
     cattail

Downspout

Rain this morning—I lay in the darkness of the bedroom
and listen to water drone off the roof, gurgle in the
downspout, patter into the hostas, the house itself as
quiet as a church. I'm reminded of a friend who recently
surrendered in her struggle, chemo against cancer.
Now, she waits. If we are linked soul to soul through our
compassion, our sameness, then we all suffer. How can I rest
so selfishly knowing her grief, her singularity, her morning
bereft of illusion? Does anxiety toss her like the wind—a
single leaf on a rain-wet tree?

stirring the rain into my coffee   June's cold spoon

Alleyway

I was too young to remember the ice truck, but I did chase
after Charlie the milkman with the kids from Ohio Street.
He kept the milk bottles chilled with blocks of ice from
the plant on 6th. They jingled and clinked in wire crates
whenever he walked them from the curb to a back door.
The truck itself was cavernous, as deep and as cool as one of
the strip pits west of town.

drifting in deep water,
a cold current embraces
my dead man's float

Occasionally, he'd take his ice pick and lop off a fistful of
shards for us to suck on. Other days he complained that
the heat melted everything too fast. He could barely get
through his delivery. Once, he shut the thick, galvanized
door in our faces without so much as a word. The cool wind
carried the scent of sour milk. One girl with rangy legs and
a mean lip said that Charlie was a prick—crazy wife or no
crazy wife. Blue jays squawked overhead, riddling the trees
with question marks. Greg stuck a grass snake in her face.

summer morning,
retreating darkness curls
inside the garden hose

Broad Leaf

Mourning is the price of love. My sister writes as we enter
the month of November. It is the month our father passed
away. I find her images in the yellow leaves, scudding
clouds, boney limbs. Our childhood yard is gated, tomato
garden overgrown with plugs of broad leaf, Dad's aluminum
ladder on the side of the house, speckled with the last paint.
Today's wind is warm, a touch of sun spots the lawn. If I
don't leave this bench, I will miss my grandson's birthday
party. His happiness is too young to turn to dust.

cardinal at the feeder,
the concrete Francis
holds an empty bowl

Turquoise Stone

I sit on the toilet chewing tobacco and thinking about reincarnation. My shoes are old. They stick out from under my jeans like duck bills. To maintain my health my wife insists I must walk 10,000 steps per day. My Indian belt has many beads, turquoise stones; a silver buckle rests on my shoe. I spit into a cracked coffee mug. When I was a boy, I had two invisible friends that I talked to in quiet moments like this. They offered advice, kept my secrets. They lived under the clothes hamper between the sink and the tub.

auction day,
the old house
drained of memory

Pearl Harbor Day

As kid I recall hearing taps being played by the ROTC.
I was a neighborhood away, but I could hear the bugle's
familiar sadness. I saluted on the front step in my Cub
Scout uniform. Today, high school students were toddlers
on 9/11. They've never known a world without cell phones,
computers, Facebook. Pearl Harbor has been swept aside
by ISIS. I can communicate with them, but it's from a
distance. I am the photograph of an uncle, brother of a
grandfather, still lonely in black and white.

estate auction,
the 'possum claims a shelf
in the empty shed

Remodeling the Cinema

I meet a man and a woman in a public restroom. He is
in a wheelchair just outside of the handicapped stall. His
wife is washing her hands. She seems flustered. Both are
embarrassed. She tells me she will be just a moment. I'm
not sure what to do. At first, I step to the urinal as usual, but
remember there's a woman at the sink. She hurries. I nod
to the man, say hello. He says hello back. She wheels him
quickly out into the lobby. The chair is new to them. They
are learning to negotiate sharp corners.

mulberry sprawl,
the starlings' purple flight
through deep shade

When I exit, he is sitting by himself, parked at an odd
angle near a *Coming Soon* cutout. I want to pat him on the
shoulder as I leave, but I don't. Sometimes less is more. He
has already had more. His wife is moving on as quickly as
possible. She is shoulder to shoulder with another woman
comparing notes on Jason Bourne. I think about them for
the rest of the evening. Throughout the many chase scenes,
he stares up at me in the bright light, his wife, drying her
hands, unable to meet my eye.

opening the field
to mouse tunnel,
the bright spade's sun

Helium Balloon

Late. No sleep. Too many thoughts rolling through my
brain. I suppose the expectations for summer. No classroom
to wear me down. No morning grind to exhaust my
thinking. I'm unleashed from earth and flying through
the ether like a helium balloon, untethered by string. A
snapped string dangling in ambient light.

night bird, a
       shadow
       perched among shadows

I've taken a pill to help me settle. Another night of trains.
The little fountain in the garden gurgles between them.
Sirens run 87th Street. More than one. Probably police.
Drama unfolds while the Monday city sleeps.

in the city's roses,
a whiskey bottle
half-filled with rain

A train locomotive throbs from the yards downtown into
the vast night of the prairie beyond. They run all night
along the old Santa Fe Trail. Steel tracks gleam. Commerce.
Consumption. Cunning. Miles from the edge of the city, a
coyote follows the darkness that winds like a river between
houses.

trash carts
at the foot of driveways,
       sidewalk
           linked to sidewalk

---

waking at 3 a.m.
how lonely
the solar lights
that run
on yesterday's sun

Butterfly Weed

His footsteps on concrete, his vision failing for months, so
much so that he walks with a stick, not a weathered, wooden
cane, but a walking stick like the kind sold at backpacking
stores, telescopic, feathered for distance. He follows the
sidewalk through his suburban neighborhood—two hills
and then down towards the creek. Overhead the cicadas
crackle and ping like thousands of dull, brass bells. He has
never noticed them so loud or so early in June. Deep purple
clouds climb over rooftops from the west. There is motion,
a flickering of the light in his weak periphery. Two white
butterflies flutter in spirals above a well-mulched orange
flower. He pauses above them. Already they are at his elbow.
The storm rises above them both. There is a tornado in the
white wings, a circular dance below the thickening sky.

lichen stretches
  gray fingers on stone
    morning's slow rain

Green River Soda

Tip's had the best magazine selection in town, something
for everybody. With my mom in the store I thumbed
through the comics, but after a Saturday double feature,
running with the Breeze brothers, I crept closer to the
Adults Only shelf, sliding past *Fish & Stream, Esquire,* and *True
Detective.* If we were quick enough, we could slip a copy of
Jugs into a *Baseball Today,* and pretend to read Mantle's stats.

in the spider's web,
   the ceiling fan
   spins today's catch

Ghosts in the Creek Bed

Sunday ends daylight savings time. I'm looking forward to the quiet darkness. The time to dedicate to other pursuits: reading, writing, long thoughts, coming winter, the days following like whispers. The Hopi traditionally had a month in deepest cold set aside for non-movement. You stayed inside by the fire, joined the earth in its time of sleep, January or its equivalent. The seasons of the earth turned the eye inward.

storm windows sealed,
the flower garden within
a ring of stones

Box of Rags

The rake has been leaning against the fence. The corners
of the yard heavy with leaf fall, windblown newsprint, paper
cups, gift wrap. Six squirrels run through the neighbor's
trees. I count their shadows, at times indistinguishable,
merging, separating, leaping into sunlight. If today were the
last day of my life, I wouldn't do anything more, except put
on my jacket and open the window.

another pot pie w/peasandcarrotsandsomethingelse

Wife and Cat

There are no curves like the curves of my wife, standing
before the mirror on a Friday morning, brushing out her
yellow hair. The cat sits on the sink, cool water running
from the faucet. He laps at it before it swirls down the drain,
quenching his night's thirst. I rest my hand on the flat of
her stomach. I know everything about her. Still, I know
nothing but what she lets me see. The cat drops to the
carpet, curls on a pile of laundry.

waking to her footsteps,
frost blossoms
melt in morning sun

Visiting Family

We made it a family weekend. I took my mother to the
cemetery. My wife did the same with her father. We had
both of them wobbling between the stones. Mother kept
saying, they've changed everything, and she'd motion
toward the vastness of the world. But I knew she meant the
caretakers, and I wondered if she thought they dug up the
dead and moved them around from year to year. But I also
knew she meant the storm that had taken out so many of
the old shade trees, leaving the spaces between the graves
sun-bleached and suburban. My wife's father, unable to
find his mother and father's graves, leaned on his walker
right above them, as right above them as yesterday's sun in
the South Pacific sky, buzzing with suicidal kamikaze—they
changed everything too—they stung from above like bees,
the whole world falling for a very long time.

sun bleached cemetery
   shadows touching
   again this spring

Oliver Claws the Door

I drove to Ace Hardware and bought a Black and Decker
Cyclone, and then, buried myself in sanding. The threshold
gaped—open-mouthed. I smoothed the ridges of his claw
marks into sloping valleys. Throughout the afternoon, the
neighbors returned from church with a sack of groceries,
a college girl jogged down the street, her ponytail bobbing
with each step. My coffee turned cold, the oily surface
speckled with dust. Now that the door was removed, Oliver
lay on the sill, whatever he had hungered for yesterday
forgotten.

late cabbage moth
flits through the marigolds,
flicker of sun

Suburban Hermit

Even after all these years of taking Paxil, anxiety leers at me from behind a potted plant. There are days when I can feel it spitting from a can of Pledge, crouching below the bed like a hairball, or seeping like a water stain under a philodendron. I keep it at bay as best I know—clean house, clean mind. But it creeps in with the cat, with the open door, with leaves in the wind.

rolling up the *Welcome* in my doormat

William Blake Saw Angels in a Tree

I saw a panda in the yard this afternoon. When I looked
closer, it turned out to be a patch of melting snow:
glaucoma, cataracts, old guy eyes. In southern Missouri, the
Spook Light dances on dirt roads, an anomaly of phosphine
and Indian legend. It's seen best after a good rain when the
bell oaks are dripping and the creeks swell with flood. A Boy
Scout troop saw its green glow stretch the width of Hornet
Road. They could count the stones in the dirt. One boy said
his shoes started to smoke.

garden mulch,
raking up the emptiness
in a snail shell

lightning at midnight,
I cannot imagine death
without this rain
the wind rising
out of the fields

Sleeping with Magnum

As an eight year old, she rode through Oklahoma into
Kansas. A train ride without parents—shipped from
aunt to aunt, mother searching for work, father taken by
pneumonia. She danced the aisle of the Pullman. She
hummed and twirled for the other passengers, laughing as
she imagined a princess riding a cloud of dust.

> one bright dress
> in the passing train
> moonless prairie

The windows at the nursing home are locked. Her son sits
with her. Each night they watch reruns of *Magnum P.I.* until
the Xanax settles and she begins to doze. Then he tells her
good night and kisses her on the forehead. Yesterday, she
didn't recognize his kiss, fought to fly from her wheelchair.
As he held her, she kicked, flailed her boney hands in the
television's Hawaiian face.

> cardinal beating
> the window
> glass sunset

Spooning

Miles away in a rest home, my mother has been lying awake in her bed. The drugs to keep her sedated have been pushed away. She knows she is not in her own home, but she cannot find the words to complain, nor can she work her legs to get up and walk away. She communicates by the alarm in her eyes, through the reports from the nurses that she cries out at night, a bird in a cat's mouth. Afternoons, I spoon her words off her chin and back between her lips.

her toe pushes the wheel chair   a circle on waxed tile

Faulkner at Christmas

Thin snow screens the lawn, coating the drive, the
sidewalks, the leaves in the dead flower garden. I step out
to unplug the Christmas lights and my nostrils contract.
Everyone is better off inside. When I listen to Christmas
carols, the slow ones, the old songs we sang as children, I
nearly weep. *White Christmas* breaks my heart. A silver bell
warms in my pocket. I need to hang it back on the door.
Even though I watch *As I Lay Dying* while wrapping presents,
there is an ache for the old music.

ice on shopping carts,
the bell ringer's squeaking
wet sneakers

Scrooge

My ears have been ringing the past two days like cicadas
have nested in them. I can't see well either, stumble
frequently. Yesterday, hanging the Christmas lights, I got
the ladder hung up in the crab apple tree. I lost my box of
staples because I didn't remember them on the hood of the
truck when I drove to the hardware store, found them on
the road after the staple gun shot blanks. I salvaged what
wasn't smashed on the street.

brushing silverfish out of a notebook of poems

Solstice

When I opened the door to let the cat out this morning, we were caught by a blast of frigid air. The cat back-pedaled into the kitchen. I snapped up the newspaper without spilling my coffee, retreated to the table. Other than the cat nosing his Kibbles, the house is still, without urgency. I have another year before I can retire, but today, I'm practicing.

snowflakes follow
first graders into class,
tether ball unwinding

Johnson County Exit

Through the soupy January mix of darkness and rain, it
is difficult to see the painted lines on the highway. I keep
the Ford at about 45 in the far lane. On-coming traffic—a
hundred eye-like lights—push from the suburbs into the
city, choreographed, keeping pace before the sun rises.

dashboard clock challenging my zen

At the bottom of the exit ramp, my headlights swing in an
arc across the construction site, a development of strip malls
and box houses. Sleet slaps the windshield. The hulk of a
bulldozer crouches in the mud.

crinoids in landscape stone   fog of diesel cloud

Blue Collar

The truck starts slowly and slides on ice at the bottom of
the driveway. The tires pop and crack across frozen slush,
headlights sweeping the road. I keep the heat off until the
engine has warmed—gloves, scarf, baseball cap, coat zipped
to my neck. About two miles down 87th Street, I flip the
switch and the first crystals of ice begin to disappear, warm
fan at the base of the windshield. My coffee is cold. I tilt the
cup to my lips.

turning on the porch light,
   old footprints darken
      last week's snow

Bone Cold

Arriving, I find the Zen Center doors locked. The front
steps bare, windswept, cold like bone. Check the calendar
for the meditation workshop. A week late. Leaning against
the wrought iron rail, breathing the winter air, diaphragm
rising, falling. One sparrow flits to the step and puffs his
feathers.

final essays graded,
sparrows prying rosehips
from snowmelt

Frozen

There is not a bird in the sky. A 9th grader walks the parking
lot before school, his face a frozen fist. He shivers from
the dead zero of the morning, hoodie pulled like a monk's
cowl. He is earlier than the others, the building itself, still
unopened. Without my key card, how long would he wait
for the door? When he shuffles past into the hallway, he
mumbles the frozen hello he saves for adults.

grasshopperinajarleaping

Key Card Dawn

Early morning geese pull the darkness behind them,
tugging the fabric of night to the west. Their voices waggle
above the rooftops, somewhere beyond my sight. They are
shadows against a larger shadow. My truck motor pings as
it cools, parking spot filled. Once more I hear the flock
before I swipe my key card through the lock. I turn. Dawn
is lifting, a slit of light, a curtain opening between the
night sky and the sleeping city. Often I am the first one
in the building. It is a time for whispering furnaces and
buzzing electric lights. There is no one to love except in
generalities: students, colleagues, bland motivations for
the good of mankind. There is a hard to reach itch in the
center of my back. I square up to an edge in the hallway
and grind the brick.

one street light caught
   in patches of ice, guessing
      shapes below snow

Chicken Feet

Driving down 39th Street in a winter rain, the stop lights,
red, the river of taillights, red, the evening sky, charcoal.
The rush hour traffic stops and starts bumper to bumper.
All windows are rolled tight except for one cracked an inch,
cigarette smoke disappearing in the rain. Foot by foot they
inch toward the intersection. Each driver alone, huddled
with his thoughts, searching ahead for a break in the traffic,
the road that leads home.

ice on wrought iron,
a window fogged with chicken
                    boiling into soup

My Irish Mother

The room is chilled by damp wind, blowing out of the
north, gray with massing cloud. I huddle over the computer
screen. In a town one hundred miles away my mother
is fading. Strokes and dementia have forced her from
wheelchair to bed. She no longer speaks a language I
recognize. She suffers nightmare visions with morphine
interludes, a chemical cocktail in her brain.

poinsettia droops
over photographs, weathered
slips of grandchildren

Yesterday, she sang in what sounded like Gaelic, or an old
woman's nonsensical word salad, a slow, ironic tone, her
family crowded in the peat smoke somewhere hardscrabble,
her blue eyes closed in an antique song. What visitor
emerges from her DNA—sister in woolen stockings, cousin
in flannel coat? What words reach her husband who has
gone ahead into the long night? She licks her lips. She rolls
her head.

crow breaking seeds
on the ice house wall,
the scattering wind

When I was a boy, she painted the moon on my bedroom
wall, a smiling cow in midflight leaping through a yellow
crescent. She told me nothing was ever as bad as it could be,
and that a dish could run away with a spoon.

Black Beads 1

At the end, Mom was living on little mouthfuls of morphine,
her breathing, labored and automatic, like she was being
pushed by some pump. Dianna said that in the morning
the birds were singing loudly. Then they stopped. Her
breathing slowed and stopped as well. She never regained
consciousness. After the service, granddaughter Ava broke
down in tears. She'd held it together until we left the
church. I told her things about heaven that sooth people,
especially kids. Things that I wish soothed me.

assisted living:
tomato vines staked
in winter wind

Black Beads 2

I went out to the strip pits to sit by a body of water and to
listen to the wind and birds. I was too restless and tired
to relax. On the way back to town, my prayer beads that
I've kept hanging on my mirror broke, dropped to the
floorboards, clattering everywhere. Even weeks later,
they keep turning up, spilling out of nowhere onto the floor
mats, seat covers, the stack of papers I haven't graded.

rolling my reflection down with the window
                meadowlark song

winter morning—
patches of old snow
litter the schoolyard
the crunch of moonlight
below my shoes

Scudding Sky

A muskrat swims the strip pit, his wake a crease in the
reflection of sky. On windy days white caps top the waves;
the muskrat retreats into the mud bank. The leaves of
poplars dance, the sky a riot of falling and rising leaves.
Crows cry against the wind, talons fastened to thin limbs.
Back in town the local football team scores in late minutes.
The ROTC cannon pops like a faraway balloon, cheers
dissipating above the bean fields. Rusted barbed wire,
looped and twined with scrub growth, connecting post to
post, stops nothing.

winter shadows:
in the heart
of the furnace a flame

Girls' Choir

A dark haired girl sits in the center of the choir room
pecking out songs on the piano. Her classmates are giggling
through study hall. Some lounge on the floor texting,
studying their phone screens. Another has isolated herself
and connects dots in an AP English assignment. The
girl at the piano returns to a fragment of a song which is
reminiscent of McCartney's "Golden Slumbers." She plays
around the melody. Maybe her song is something else,
something more modern. Nevertheless, the energy in the
room settles, girl linked to girl at 10 a.m.

slits of sunlight
through winter blinds, dancing
blue fingernails

Tool Shed

A wasp taps the window pane while I read through a green
spiral notebook that I find in the back of a filing cabinet,
now relegated to tool storage, hammers, jars of nails,
sandpaper, glue, graduate school notes for a seminar on the
Romantics. Scattered throughout the pages are fragments
of poems, lines that I thought were poetic, lofty, thick
with Shelley. No wonder they sputtered, died like a fouled
garden tiller, throttle-rich, spark-dulled. So hard to find a
poem still fresh. Now, as I try to capture the taste of a freshly
picked tomato—it is somewhere between micro-waved
cheese dip and sautéed morels.

> burying half a rabbit
> in the garden mulch,
> the shovel's shine

Through the Screen Door

For the longest time, nothing moves except a single
cicada, short, staccato chirps erupting occasionally in the
maple. Stillness gloves the afternoon to the elbows. Then
the postal worker's truck creeps up the block, stopping
at each driveway with the clank of a box lid, thrum of
an accelerator, a squeak of brakes. Each sound separate,
distinct. Someone waits for good news, a letter, a blue moth
in August.

below the bleached sky
one sheet
drying on the clothesline

Temple of the Ford Ranger

Seeking refuge off a busy street, a parking lot in the rain.
Sitting under the trees in the back of the lot, cell phone off,
window down, rain falls from the walnuts onto the truck
cab—the metallic drip, the call of the doves, the rubber
swish of tires on 95th Street list away into the silence. It is
as if there is a hollow spot in the morning, empty like the
inside of a maraca, resting in the mariachi's hand. For the
first time this morning I put my finger on all that is song.

rain drop
splashing into rain drop
    into rain drop

Charleston Midnight

A mother is awake, unable to sleep without Xanax. She rises
from bed and walks the house, pausing at the back door
to watch the storm sweep the patio, and then at the front
door to see if her stone retaining wall is being washed into
the street. It is two a.m. She should be sleeping, or at least,
listening to the storm through the window. The neighbor's
sycamore is twice as high as her wooden house, highest
limbs tossing crazily. If she owned a pistol, she would fire
back into the clouds, into the cracking branches, into the
heart of hate.

window light pasted
behind a curtain of rain,
wind shadow

First Seed

My wrestling team lifted a Bible from a motel in 1975, the cover red with white lettering. School colors. At the State Regionals they broke a television, collapsed a bed, and picked fights at the 7-11. Forty years later, the Gideon is still the first thing I unpack at the beginning of the school year. My desk is stuffed with talismans, a broken stopwatch, a detention slip, a whistle. Even this beat up Bible, lifted while they emptied their pockets to pay the damages—binding loose, pages yellowed. No one the wiser.

> iris in the rain
> thumbprint
> on your photograph

Cleaning Out the Rock Garden

I've cut back on my paroxetine. Probably, that is why the
depression returns. Stone by stone, pocket by pocket, it's
not fair for the people around me, wife, children, friends. I
should re-up the dosage, medicate balance. I had planned
to rise above this on my own. That was my hope. But I'm
not able to keep this flood levied behind meditation. I
dog paddle, tread with heavy legs, sink like a concrete St.
Francis.

garden stone
cracked from the long freeze,
    empty snail shells

Then too, if I'm talking physiology, brain chemistry, and
the serotonin isn't present, then hell, it'll never get better
without meds. That's the downside to turning stones, the
upside to finding...

wild onion
raked up with winter leaves
    among hyacinth fingers

Stonecrop

An abandoned road bends downhill. Once a railroad access,
it twists, rutted and wash-boarded, to the valley. The thick
tangle of forest canopies what little road remains. Early
signs of leaf change splatter the tops of the trees—wearied
yellow, mottled brown, splashed red. The season's frost
works from the sky downwards to the roots. The cell phone
vibrates a text: poetry reading in Westport cancelled.

tapping the awning,
    the moth's flight
    in and out of rain

More reliable are the sighing trees, the distant woodpeckers
and the insistent crickets. Stonecrop, scattered across the
rocks, blooms beyond summer's end, as oblivious to man
as stars, snags the rocky soil with tenacious roots, waiting
the occasional rain, following the sun, cultivated by wind
and bees. Three vultures ride the air currents into full sun.
They tilt, spin on wingtips. Crows in the distant hedgerow
applaud the solitude, the old voice speaking.

tangled honeysuckle,
    a bicycle
    chained to bicycles

Green Painted Walls

Nervous breakdown. Just thought I'd write the words
down. Anyone who has suffered from an anxiety disorder
knows what I'm talking about. Looking backwards, it looms
as a possibility, an opportunity maybe that somehow you
missed, or not, sitting by a steam radiator below a window,
institutionalized at last, hands folded in lap, relaxed with
tranquilizers. All is flaccid, like sponge, like spaghetti, like
sandwich cheese. At the funny farm with nothing more
to prove. Either everything is funny or nothing is funny.
Why don't you comb your hair, lovely lady? Put on lipstick.
Mascara darker than the rings below your eyes. Sit with me
here at the window. We don't have to talk. It would be better
if we didn't. Let's pick the loose threads from our pajamas.
Let's draw self-portraits of the strangers we've become.

mirror, your lips taste like glass

Wall Dogs

An air of aloofness follows him like the scent of turpentine. A
half-smoked cigar punctuates his mouth. This afternoon he stops
on the sidewalk outside of the 311 Club, chewing his Roi-Tan.
He studies our fresh, multi-colored trim, turns the cigar with
his fingertips. His signature corners most of the signs in town.
We know his truck, eye the progress of each new commission.
Summer mornings find him on the east side of Broadway;
evenings on the west side—at night, still on his ladder, he paints
by street light.

nighthawks above the street lights   dive for insects

We specialize in interior enamel and intricate exterior trim.
The country club passes our names like business cards. But the
old sign painter with the curly hair and speckled horn rims is
legendary to us. His deft brush strokes and keen eye decorate
more than a quarter of a century of town. We hang on the drift of
his cigar smoke. Artistry, whether high on a brick storefront, or
on 1930s cove molding, demands a formidable love.

narrow ribbon of shade   dog in the doorway snaps at his shadow

The Story Begins with a Dog

The tears from the veteran came when he described the death of his small dog, the cancer he wishes he had caught earlier, before it was too late for treatment. This is his story, the one he has agreed to tell. There are others we can only imagine still buried in Afghanistan with unexploded ordinances, buried in hillsides near the caves, the ravines of war. I sense there is more to be told, maybe about the dog, maybe about the sun bleached village, the dusty camp, Humvees passing through a wire gate, dark-haired children selling DVDs, burner phones, Campbell's soup. Something is hidden, maybe an IED, a corpse on the roadside, a spinning tire on a Toyota pickup. There is more here to meet the eye than what is seen through a cracked windshield.

summer dust devil,
a hornet climbs his mountain
of pistachio shells

clouds thread
the mountain pass
—the fog
a scarf
twirling in wind

Brushing Latex on Mrs. Ford's Second Story

I paint an old house on West Kansas, ladder propped on
the porch roof as I stretch to the upper eaves, sunlight in
the catalpas. Mist roils like wings, like loosened feathers.
With bucket in hand, I lean from the rungs and touch the
highest peak, the brush marks of yesterday's painter etched
in the old lead-base like fossils, a twist of bristles, invisible
until today. There is something old in the air, an antique
song, a whistling. Mrs. Ford makes coffee this morning. She
insists the new paint shines like it did in 1945.

the paperboy's arc
smacks porch after porch,
dove calling to dove

At the Trading Post Bridge

A dozen cranes stand in the flood waters. They are as stoic as stone statues. Eighteen wheelers roar down the highway. The berm of the road like a ribbon cutting the water, trucks nervous with deadlines, fast food, livestock, refrigerated milk. They drive into the same wind that keeps the wild birds still, bones and footprints, radios and country music. Songs sing of what is forgotten, what is remembered in stillness and in flight. A jake brake roars on the curve.

in the bridge shadow,
a beer bottle
polished to stone

Orion's Belt

The backyard gate swings shut in the middle of the night.
I have been up for an hour in a darkened bedroom when
I hear it. The sound is too deliberate for stealth, for a
sneaking thief. I flip on a lamp and take my water bottle
down the stairs. Someone has been walking through the
yard in the dark hours. I imagine them standing alone
below one of the trees, listening to the little wind that blows
warm out of the south. A few stars are visible between the
branches, the moon behind shadows.

paper cup discarded
in the emptiness
between stars

Spring Snow

Several months ago Aunt Dee gave me a letter that she found in grandma's things. A letter from mom to grandma, dated March 18, 1952. She was writing from New York while dad was at Ft. Dix. Mom was 22 and pregnant for the first time. She wrote like a girl in love, missing her soldier husband. She had two names picked out for the baby—Deborah Lee and Alfred Jr.—I guess I know how that turned out. I realized while reading that this was the first I'd ever heard my mother speak with the voice of a woman who wasn't yet a mother. She wrote like a girl, used the word "swell," described New York snow as "glistening into spring"—with perfect penmanship. She was just getting to know my father...he was a great "guy," and they hadn't had a fight in an entire year.

public library steps
a veteran cradles Tolstoy
against his stump

Home Opener

It was the coldest day for baseball I'd ever encountered. At
one point my teeth were chattering as I watched Jack play
ball at the Little K behind the center field wall. Finally, out
of the wind at our seats, I slid a hand warmer under my
shirt next to my neck to stop shivering. The highlight was
watching batting practice. Jack was the only kid on the Pepsi
Porch so several players tossed him balls. He walked away
with four, which is basically unheard of. One of them he
actually snagged with his own glove. Paulino, the pitcher
who tossed the ball, gave him a thumbs-up.

rain delay, spitting
sunflower shells
over the right field wall

Shooting Hoops for Beer

Shooting hoops behind the filling station on Prospect—
Gunner Delmont takes the feed from Sneaky King,
elbowing until the blood flows, playing tough all Sunday
afternoon, gray sweatshirts stained like oily concrete.
Old school kicks—toe to toe, any tandem with game and
five bucks to stake are taken on. Young women compete
with blue jays, squabbling beside the Pontiacs, between
Buicks, men they knew by name, by reputation, hoppers,
dealers from the corner, the playground fence tangled with
yellowed Virginia creeper and pale sun.

wild geese circle
Columbus Park—yellow leaves
twirling in bus exhaust

A series of linoleum cuts hangs in a college gallery, a study
of streets left behind, boys and girls dulled by the men and
women they've become. The same broken branch hangs
above the house. The palm reader's sign fades in the front
window.

Thieves at Night

Last night the wind came up out of the south. I could
hear it lifting the trees in the yard and banging against
the aluminum storm window. I pulled the blanket higher
after punching the pillow into its original thickness. The
house rested in stillness, dark rooms spilling into the darker
hallway. My wife, sunken in an Ambien oblivion, didn't stir.
Rain followed, splattering in gusts against the thin glass.
A baseball bat leaned against the bedroom doorjamb. In
tonight's dim light it appeared small, even foolish against
a formidable intruder. A good roof, caulked windows, a
serviced furnace—the digital clock cuts the darkness.

mom's bud vases
yellowed greetings tied
with florist ribbon

Tailgating at the Last Supper

for H. Who Thought Victorians Humorous for Using Initials
Rather than Last Names

G brought several six packs of Czech beer, iced in a
Styrofoam cooler. We drank and told stories around H's
bed, wagering that inside his skin, he was hearing, smiling,
laughing his ass off. M said later as we drove to town that he
kept seeing H in the image of El Greco's *Christ on the Cross*,
sallow, open-eyed at the end, embraced by sorrow, by love. I
pictured small children clambering up the Skull and sitting
with him, rubbing his arms, his chest, washing his feet with
their fingertips, running their hands through his hair.

heart-shaped stone
in the gravel drive, vines
    climbing a mailbox

Still up from a late night—eating 99 cent sanchos from
Taco Station at 3:00 a.m.—M passed out in the cab of his
truck. Walnut husks, heavy with rain, drop onto the hood—
salsa, shreds of cheese, and lettuce—weary as a steamed
tortilla, eating to suck up the alcohol, easing the transition
to morning. We never once spoke the word death. Even
driving home, we kept it out of the conversation. Night
whispered in the solitude of roadside ditches, in the pools
of rain water, in the floating leaves.

magenta blossoms
in the myrtle, secret twig
    of walking stick

old photograph
of my father
the watch on his wrist
keeping time
in a box on my desk

Monofilament Whiskers

Dying stinks on a cat. His preening has stopped, no longer licking his paws or cleaning his coat. He slinks and crowds toward the milk plate, bones like loose bundles of fishing poles, hooked claws, sinker eyes, a jar of blood bait hardened to paste. Demanding privacy, he disappears into quiet corners of the garden. At night, he is just a small swell of moonlight behind the rhododendron. In the morning his face is turned upwards like he was searching the sky.

slow rain before dawn,
owl calling beyond
the churchyard pines

Grub Worm

The rain that has been building all morning begins to tap
the window. The sash, raised to allow the garden into the
bedroom, is enough of a poem for anyone. Ink can only
imitate these first drops, the quiet within the curtained
room, the breeze kneading muscle, the drizzling calm. Blue
jays swing through the sycamore. Already yellowed, its heavy
leaves, thickened at the stem, fall like birds.

the spider's midnight
web collects rain drops, mist
of late tomatoes

The Styrofoam of Stuff

I've been sitting in this office all morning, trying like hell
to keep my eyes open. I've even closed them for twenty
minutes on the little couch in the cubicle. I found several
pieces of Double Bubble gum and wedged the stone-hard
cubes into my mouth. I've swallowed two cups of really bad
coffee. I've fingered a dip of Skoal under my lower lip. If I
had tea bags, I'd put them on my eyes and let them soak in
caffeine.

earbuds dangling,
    motion sensors
click to twilight

Somewhere on the Atlantic, a ship is heaving in the waves.
The salt spray is running down the faces of those who sail
her. The closer they get to land, the more the seagulls
scream overhead. No one onboard complains about tired
eyes. I dose myself with Refresh Tears. Somewhere in
Kansas, make-believe dolphins crest the surface of a wheat
field. They are eager to leap, eager to dive.

half a bagel
    on a napkin—
poppy seed spray

Across the Wooden Fence

I love mornings when the thunder rumbles and the lightning flashes and the cool breeze lifts the curtains into the bedroom. It is a mantra for me, one that says let go, nothing more is expected, listen and sleep. Rain splatters the deck. The squirrels run the top of the fence. The pear's white blossoms dip with storm-weight. There is a truth to simplicity. If I begin to list all that I know for certain, it would begin with an observation of where I'm sitting with paper and pen.

blue deepens
in the columbine's
wet throat

Light in the Back of the House

The cat will not shut up. He has whined since waking.
Three times I've crawled out of bed to see what he wants,
filled his bowl twice, added fresh water, given him treats.
Still he complains. The temperatures will drop today into
single digits. The wind has picked up. I can hear it in the
eaves; see it in the bare branches of the dogwood. The gate
to George's fence swings on its hinges. No one enters. No
one leaves. Gray mornings help me focus. A hawk has come
from the creek. He sits in the lower branches of the maple.
I haven't noticed him before—in from the fields to hunt,
his talons, curved around a limb, creasing the bark.

frozen to the bird bath
the twitter of leaves
    locked in ice

Passing Period

Classes are changing, and although I made it to the door quickly,
I am beaten by a teacher from across the hall. He pees slowly,
washes his hands front and back, dries them carefully with
too many paper towels. I hear him pumping them from the
dispenser the way I used to jack-up my BB gun. Then there's
another pause, one that I cannot account for. His hand should
be turning the door handle, unlatching the dead bolt. My guess
is that he combs his thick hair, checks his nostrils for hangers,
tongues the gaps between his teeth. In a moment the bell will
ring. My students will be in class, milling between their desks,
shooting Instagrams into cyber space. The principal walks the
hall with his clipboard. As I round the corner, he scribbles a
note.

old coach   dribbling the basketball through the gym's twilight

Beige Jesus

From where I'm sitting on the third floor, the white steeple
of a church stands stark and cold against the blue sky. It
is as severe as a spear, a white phallus. Nothing warm or
feminine about it. No hand-hewn stone. No greening vines.
Traffic gleams in the afternoon, windshields, metallic paint,
flashing chrome. All positioned within painted lines on
polished black pavement. Even the children's playground,
carefully slanted behind the chain link fence, is regimented
like a parade formation, swings, monkey bars in rows. From
my window the surrounding neighborhood stretches to the
interstate, each rooftop the same brown, apex angled to
apex, rising out of canyons of beige.

the scent of turned fields—early spring in terra cotta pots

Pine Tree Morning

Students write rough drafts over Blake's two Chimney
Sweepers. It's not an easy assignment, forces them to think,
even though we've discussed the direction of the poems
and how they relate to *Songs of Innocence and Experience.* The
morning is gray and quiet. Almost as if snow is expected,
coming in on low clouds, at first, materializing as if from
nothing in the cold air, and then, in sweeping white dust on
the highway. If I were to believe everything I'm told about
existence, I would only have to make one initial choice,
and after that it would be enough to follow—the sun or the
moon. Instead there is this long twilight which encapsulates
us like a cloud, but then comes a red bird, a lone headlight
on a country road, a soughing pine.

in the hush before snow
the rooftop's…
      starling ellipses

---

snow falling
through rush hour traffic
taillights linked
by the single thought
of home

Stone Fence

Sitting by the Little Sugar. The green water rolling below
the hanging trees. Pool drop. Pool drop. Rounding a quiet
bend. Small cabin on tall legs, flood stilts. Picture window
overlooking the trees, the running stream. Whip-o-wills
at night. Wind in the tops of the trees. Little on the trail.
Dappled shade. Lichen gray rock. Looking in my heart for
someplace other than these four walls. I lean backwards
into the past for inspiration. The smell of fallen leaves
on the forest floor. Deer print sunk into the creek bank.
Up from the water's edge into the trees, up again to the
bluff trail. Then on back along the creek. The high trail of
overturned leaves, skunk cabbage, centipede. All we follow
is left behind.

leaves behind leaves   beyond branches

Kayaking the Upper Buffalo

Whitewater rainbows in spray, pool dropping between willows, river birch, driftwood—three buzzards, droop-shouldered, perch in ash. Popping lid on tin of sardines, one bird lifts immediately into flight, begins to turn circles on wingtip. Sun splashes off standing waves, dampens limestone, dries, dampens. Mayapple umbrellas below blackjack oaks. Blue-tailed skink skitters into patch of sun.

drifting hawk,
a broken shadow
circles the bluff

Metal Bailed Bucket

I dug his surrealistic canvas from the trash. The apartment above the grocery closed, cleaned for deposit. Old broom. Floor mop. Black plastic bags, twist-tied. Empty beer cans. Windex bottles. A year of art study. Wheatfield below blue sky. Fingernail clipper flying west. Tree line of hedge, a cottonwood in the faraway. Another of fried eggs sliding off a threshold onto steps opening onto a desert of cactus bloom and spike. A blow torch in red. Still life. Fruitless. The wheat field and clippers hang in my classroom forty years after I rescued them. Semester by semester, painting students have cleaned their own apartments, left much of themselves in trash heaps, in dumpsters, in forgotten brush strokes.

playground voices
      climb the sky
      on blue jay wings

Last Float Trip on the Gasconade

Rain and sleet pelted the crocus, popped off the flotsam of early spring. Our john boat foundered, turned sideways. We bailed with a plastic Clorox jug until it, too, escaped beyond reach. The boat swamped before it capsized, spilling us in a willow jungle, the flat bottom inverted, disappearing behind a snag of limb fall, bobbers, fishing line, Styrofoam floats. No one could say we hadn't seen it coming, the water and the boat becoming one. We paddled in small circles, gasping at the cold, the flood we called tomorrow, spinning us away from each other like fallen leaves.

echo of her footsteps   before closing the door

Swimming Deer

A young buck swims the center of Shoal Creek in flood
stage. Rains have pummeled the hills for two days. Now,
sunlight like yellow flowers patchworks the timber, crosses
the lapping waves, climbs the bluff. The buck bobs in and
out of dappled shade, felted antlers green in early sun.
Spring run-off carries him through the park and under the
distant highway bridge. Hawks catch the April wind, rise
quickly into the fresh blue. All that ever was, or will be, is
now.

dogwood spray
in gray timber, daffodils
clutched in landfill

Hunting Morels

I'm beginning to feel a little relief. I noticed a second ago
that I could breathe differently, like with the thought of
poetry, silence between breaths. Kristin walked into my
classroom with a photograph of fresh morels. That's exactly
what I'm thinking of—discovery. For the past few weeks,
months, no, a year since my mother's stroke, I've been
pressed between two stones, job and hospice. Now that
mom's struggle has ended, a desire flickered to walk along
Mill Creek. In a certain sense, everything I've undertaken
lately has been endured. I'm referring to family events,
social engagements, work without joy. A moment ago, I felt
this lift just a bit. I recalled a wooded hillside at the water's
edge. Tom said, look for morels when the oak leaves are the
size of a squirrel's ear.

early spring,
walking the sidewalk
into forsythia spray

Black Bear

Rain pools in bear tracks. Our food, hung in a black tarp, drips all night. At ten thousand feet rain mixes with wisps of snow, cloud layers upon cloud. There is a hot shower, water heated by a wood stove. We crowd on rough pallets in a small board enclosure, waiting our turn, hoping someone stokes the fire for the last in line. I crouch on the mountainside with my back to a stump, poncho pulled over my hat, nylon draped like a curtain over my shoulders. The hat's brim funnels the rain beyond my boots like a downspout. When the clouds part, a patch of lighter gray rides above the darker gray. A broad winged bird, maybe an eagle, pulls the wind behind him and closes the sky.

bacon sizzling
in the ranger's cabin,
rain in my skillet

high on Mt. Sneffels
hikers pass in the overcast
like clouds themselves—
no way up or down
without disappearing

Acknowledgments

After the Pause: "Black Beads 2," "Spooning"
Akitsu Quarterly: "Black Bear," "Tool Shed"
Allegro Poetry Journal: "Sleeping with Magnum"
Amaryllis: "Girls Choir"
A Quiet Courage: "Blue Collar," "Oliver Claws the Door"
Beechwood Review: "Ghosts in the Creek Bed," "Solstice"
Ink in Thirds: "Beige Jesus"
Cattails: "Butterfly Weed," "Temple of the Ford Ranger"
Contemporary Haibun Online: "Broad Leaf," "Death Is
      a Sneeze," "Faulkner at Christmas," "Helium Balloon"
Down in the Dirt: "Turquoise Stone"
Eunoia: "At the Trading Post Bridge," "Charleston Midnight"
Failed Haiku: "First Seed," "Scrooge"
Frogpond: "Tailgating at the Last Supper"
The Galway Review: "Box of Rags," "Chicken Feet," "My
      Irish Mother," "Suburban Hermit"
Haibun Today: "Bone Cold," "Spring Snow"
The Jawline Review: "Across the Wooden Fence," "Cleaning
      Out the Rock Garden," "Visiting Family"
Jersey Devil Press: "high on Mt. Sneffels," "poncho
      over my head"
Melancholy Hyperbole: "The Styrofoam of Stuff"
Modern Haiku: "Frozen," "On the Chicopee Spur"
One Sentence Poems: "winter morning"
Plum Tree Tavern: "Grub Worm," "Swimming Deer"
Poetry Breakfast: "Johnson County Exit," "Kayaking
      the Upper Buffalo"
Red Eft Review: "Whiskers"
Revolution John: "Thieves at Night"
Shamrock: "Wife and Cat," "Wrist Slap"
Skylark: "snow falling"
Sonic Boom: "Passing Period"

Star 82 Review: "Key Card Dawn"
Turtle Island Quarterly: "Stonecrop"
Thirteen Ways: "Light in the Back of the House"
Undertow Tanka Review: "old photograph,"
        "waking at 3 a.m."
Yellow Chair Review: "Green River Soda"